KELLY FLANAGAN

TRUE
COMPANIONS
STUDY GUIDE

FIVE SESSIONS ON HOW TO SHOW UP IN

YOUR MOST IMPORTANT RELATIONSHIPS

An imprint of InterVarsity Press
Downers Grove, Illinois

InterVarsity Press
P.O. Box 1400, Downers Grove, IL 60515-1426
ivpress.com
email@ivpress.com

InterVarsity Press® is the book-publishing division of InterVarsity Christian Fellowship/USA®, a movement of students and faculty active on campus at hundreds of universities, colleges, and schools of nursing in the United States of America, and a member movement of the International Fellowship of Evangelical Students. For information about local and regional activities, visit intervarsity.org.

While any stories in this book are true, some names and identifying information may have been changed to protect the privacy of individuals.

Published in association with Creative Trust Literary Group LLC, 320 Seven Springs Way, Suite 250, Brentwood, TN 37027, www.creativetrust.com.

Author photo by Grot Imaging Studio, grotis.com.

Cover design and image composite: David Fassett
Interior design: Jeanna Wiggins
Images: dust scratches on a black background: © golubovy / iStock / Getty Images Plus
    botanical illustration: © bauhaus1000 / DigitalVison Vectors / Getty Images
    white texture background: © R.Tsubin / Moment Collection / Getty Images

ISBN 978-0-8308-4770-9 (print)
ISBN 978-0-8308-4771-6 (digital)

Printed in the United States of America ♾

Library of Congress Cataloging-in-Publication Data
A catalog record for this book is available from the Library of Congress.

P 25 24 23 22 21 20 19 18 17 16 15 14 13 12 11 10 9 8 7 6 5 4 3 2 1
Y 41 40 39 38 37 36 35 34 33 32 31 30 29 28 27 26 25 24 23 22 21

CONTENTS

WELCOME TO COMPANION CAMP

Live the questions now.
Perhaps you will then gradually, without noticing it,
live along some distant day into the answer.

RAINER MARIA RILKE

T RUE COMPANIONS is a book for everyone. It's right there in the subtitle: *A Book for Everyone About the Relationships That See Us Through*. That's true of this study guide, as well. I've structured these five sessions so that you can work through them with a friend or a bunch of friends, with your spouse or lifelong partner, with a class or your church small group, with a parent or a child or a sibling, and even, simply, with yourself. Before we go any further, though, I would encourage you to stop thinking of this as a study guide.

Think of this, instead, as Companion Camp.

I first used that phrase—Companion Camp—at a marriage retreat. The beginning of every marriage retreat is fraught with tension. Some couples are there to save their marriage, and the retreat weekend is a last-ditch effort. They've tried couples counseling already, and it has not worked, so the stakes are high. They tend to feel a decent amount of despair, and they are skeptical about the sustainability of any hope the weekend may give them.

Some couples are there not because their marriage is failing but because it is stagnating. For them, the weekend is an effort to take their marriage to the next level. They feel determined and committed, but they are a little skeptical, too, probably because they've already tried to find this "other level" everyone speaks of, with nothing to show for it.

On the other hand, some couples are there as a celebration of their marriage. For them, all is well and they are simply seeking a little time away to rest, relax, and enrich their relationship. Nevertheless, they too feel a bit of trepidation at the beginning of the weekend because, deep down, they worry the retreat is going to stir up issues in the marriage that need not be stirred up.

So, yeah, fraught with tension.

I was leading a marriage retreat of about thirty couples, and I'm guessing the couples were pretty evenly divided among these three types. We assembled on a Saturday morning, and sixty sets of eyes stared at me with equal parts caution and distrust. The question written on those faces was clear: "What are you about to do to us?" The first thing I did to them was to read the introduction to *True Companions*, including excerpts like this one:

In her Pulitzer Prize–winning novel, *Gilead*, Marilynne Robinson writes, "The moon looks wonderful in this warm evening light, just as a candle flame looks beautiful in the light of morning. Light within light. . . . It seems to me to be a metaphor for the human soul, the singular light within the great general light of existence. Or it seems like poetry within language. Perhaps wisdom within experience. Or marriage within friendship and love." What if marriage is a singular light within the great general light of *companionship*, but we keep trying to turn it into the big light itself? What if uncovering the secrets to a stellar marriage isn't as important as finding our way to the truths at the heart of true companionship?

When I finished reading, I looked up and said, "So, you can quit thinking of this as a marriage retreat. Instead, I want you to think of it as Companion Camp." The shift in energy was palpable. You could see hope animate some eyes. You could see weight lift from some shoulders. You could see tenderness smooth out some brows.

How do you fix your relationship? That question is riddled with so much pressure and anxiety and stress it is best left unasked. Here's an entirely different question: *How do you show up as the best companion you can be in your most important relationships?* The answers to that question can take the pressure off, instill hope rather than fear, and make your relationships more joyful and less stressful. So, right here, right now, I want to say the same thing to you:

Welcome to Companion Camp.

Camp is both entertaining *and* challenging, playful *and* meaningful. We are going to talk about the things that are most important to your relationships, but we are not going to talk about them in ways that leave you feeling raw and exposed and undone. We are going to have fun times and hopeful conversations and, in the end, you will have a new vision for how you can best show up in every relationship that matters to you.

Welcome to Companion Camp!

IOU: THE PATTERN OF TRUE CONNECTION

On a warmer than usual autumn afternoon, I had a weekly mentoring meeting scheduled with one of the therapists I employ. I suggested we spend the hour walking and talking in order to enjoy the weather. He happily agreed. Then, several minutes into our walk, I asked him to stop at the ATM with me. His agreement was a little less enthusiastic. As we walked away from the ATM, he asked me if he could give me some feedback. I said yes. He reminded me that a couple weeks earlier we'd done another of my errands during one of our meetings. He told me he wants to become the best therapist he can be, and having my full attention during our supervision meetings would help him to do so.

The urge arose within me to respond immediately and defensively.

Instead, I stopped myself, and I took a moment instead to remember the fundamental pattern that underpins all healthy human growth and connection: inward (I), then outward (O), then upward (U). I call it the IOU pattern. In that moment of reflection, I realized I was tempted to go quickly outward, toward him, offering an impulsive reaction, and skipping the first step in all true human connection: going inward to be with oneself.

4

The inward journey is always one of self-reflection. It takes us into the swirl of our thoughts and emotions, our impulses and compulsions, our past that feels so present, our present that feels so passing, and our future that feels so opaque. The inward journey brings our attention to the rushing river of human experience within us but, rather than jumping into the river to be carried away, we stand at the banks, watching it flow by, learning from what we observe. This kind of contemplation is at the heart of the inward journey.

The outward journey, as I define it, is the lateral movement toward another person. It consists of the one-on-one interactions that make up most of our days. It's the murmuring of lovers, the negotiating of partners, the conversing among two friends, the parenting of a child, and the debating of opponents. It makes up the bulk of the fighting and the socializing we do in the world. Even when you are at a large party or social gathering, most of your interactions will happen in pairs. You will talk to one person at a time, one after the other, all night long. This is the outward journey.

The upward journey is the movement toward anything bigger and more transcendent than the day-to-day paired interactions that constitute most of our lives. This journey often begins as we identify with and connect with our immediate and extended families. It expands to include our larger group affiliations, our common inheritance with all of humanity, and our experience of the presence of God. Some people call God their higher power or the universe or essence or spirit or the greater good, among other things. These are all attempts to describe the ultimate destination of the upward journey. Personally, my destination is Jesus.

Regrettably, most of us tend to fixate our life and our love on only one of these three journeys, to the neglect of the others, and each type of fixation comes with its own drawbacks. For instance, those who focus exclusively on the inward journey almost always fall into the unfortunately named trap of navel-gazing. They can go to counseling for years without ever seeing a payoff in their relationships outside of the therapy room. In the words of theologian Richard Rohr, "People who avoid intimacy are always, and I mean always, imprisoned in a small and circular world. *Intimacy is the only gateway into the temple of human or divine love.*" The outward journey is the bridge between the inward journey and the upward journey.

By contrast, people who focus almost exclusively on the outward journey toward other people—without first going on an inward journey of self-reflection—can do great damage to their relationships. For example, having not experienced self-love and self-acceptance via the inward journey, they demand a kind of love and acceptance from each companion that no companion can give. Furthermore, by ignoring the call of the upward journey, their relationships become the be-all and end-all of their existence, and the pressure on those relationships to satisfy transcendent longings can crush them.

Finally, when we skip the hard but good work of our inward and outward journeys and focus only on the upward journey, our faith and vocation and outreach to the rest of humanity are often characterized by arrogance, self-righteousness, judgment, exclusion, and control. Without first being formed into truly loving people on the first two steps of the journey, our attempts to love God, the planet, or humanity in general ring out as jarringly as a clanging cymbal. We need all three journeys: inward, outward, then upward. IOU. It is important for us to honor this pattern of growth and connection over the course of our lives, but also in each and every relationship and, indeed, in each and every moment.

Such as an unusually warm autumn afternoon with your employee.

As the two of us walked back toward the office, I paused before responding. I went inward before I went outward, and on that inward journey I became aware of several things. First, I noticed my defensiveness—I'd prefer for my employees to think that I lead them perfectly. Second, I realized he was right—I was giving my to-do list more attention than I was giving to him. Third, I noticed an appreciation for his desire to be the best therapist he can be—I admire striving for excellence wherever I find it. Finally, I found myself impressed by his courage to be so vulnerable with me.

So, having discovered these things on my inward journey, I went on the outward journey toward him. I told him I appreciated and admired him. I told him he'd have my full attention from now on. In that moment, I knew I needed to go upward with these insights as well. This wasn't just about my interactions with one employee. It was about the way I was showing up to all my people: my family, my friends, my team at work, pedestrians and motorists, even God. I was letting them tag along on my journey, rather than truly entering into a shared journey *with* them. I decided I want to show up differently to my *life*. Inward, outward, upward.

IOU.

This can be the pattern of every moment, if we choose it, and this is the pattern of *True Companions*. Part one of the book is called "Grow Quiet: Befriending Your Loneliness," and it is about the necessary journey inward to encounter our loneliness and learn what to do with it. Part two is called "Grow Strong: Embracing Your Struggle," and it is about learning how to balance going inward with going outward, in order to let go of our long-standing relationship protections so we can connect with each of our companions more authentically. Finally, Part three is called "Grow Old: Cherishing Your Time," and it is about living the upward journey through transcendent things like time and aging and hardship and death, in order to identify and live out our priorities in a way most consistent with our highest values.

Inward, outward, then upward.

IOU: THE STRUCTURE OF EACH SESSION

The IOU pattern is also reflected in this study guide. Each of these five sessions invites you into a brief period of self-reflection after reading through the content for that session (inward), a paired interview at the beginning of each group session (outward), and a larger group discussion to conclude each session (upward). If you are doing this study in a group, this means you will want to make time for the inward, self-reflective exercise prior to your weekly meeting. I'd also encourage you to spend some time reflecting on—and perhaps even answering— the outward, paired-interview questions prior to your group meeting. It's not essential, but it will help you get the most out of your time with each other.

Of course, if you are going through this study by yourself, you will still be able to benefit from each of these three kinds of exercises. Specifically, you can engage the paired interview and the group questions in each session as additional opportunities for reflection and contemplation. In this way, your inward journey here at Companion Camp will be exceptionally deep and rich.

Now, let's take a closer look at the three kinds of exercises included in each session.

Inward. You may be tempted to rush through these questions on your own. Try to slow down. Good questions will take you into places you don't normally go, to discover things you don't normally see. This requires the freedom that space provides. Schedule at least thirty minutes on your calendar for each inward reflection. Protect the space so you won't be interrupted. Turn off your device notifications. Create the silence necessary for the inward journey.

Outward. Every paired interview you do during this study will follow the same format, though the questions you ask of each other will differ with each session. Each paired interview will take a total of about thirty minutes, with each partner interviewing the other for fifteen minutes. If you have an uneven number of group members on any given day, you can have three group members do the interview together and pare down the interview time for each member to ten minutes. Of course, you can also choose to answer these questions ahead of time and simply discuss them as a group, without pairing off. However, I'd encourage you to do the paired interviews if possible, as they can be an effective way to harness the power of the outward journey. Here are the guidelines for a paired interview:

- Pair off in whatever way you prefer.

- Once you have paired off, choose a Partner A and a Partner B.

- Partner A interviews Partner B for fifteen minutes.

- Remember, this is more like an interview than a conversation. Even if you know each other well, try to approach the interview as if you're meeting each other for the first time. Be curious. Partner A, take note of anything particularly interesting or inspiring.

- After fifteen minutes, Partner A can affirm Partner B with one thing they heard or noticed that they appreciated the most.

- Then switch roles, with Partner B interviewing Partner A, following the same guidelines as above, and once again concluding with an affirmation of something Partner B particularly appreciated about the interview.

When you begin the larger group discussion afterward, you will have a chance to share—with your partner's permission—anything important you took away from the interview that you think might also be of value to the group.

If you are working through these five sessions with a long-time companion, you might be tempted to think you already know all the answers. After all, in relationships, our conversations fall into ruts. Our conflict plays out according to the same script almost every time. We think we know what comes next because we do! However, new questions are going to give rise to new conversations and answers and insights. So, before you begin, I'd encourage you to look at each other and say, "I'm looking forward to being surprised by what we discover in the midst of this study." In fact, say it at the beginning of every session!

Upward. Having completed the paired interview (or a discussion of the paired interview questions if you reviewed them as a group), create a bridge to the upward portion of the study by taking a few minutes for group members to share what they appreciated most or what was most valuable to them from the paired interview. When everyone has had an opportunity to share (though of course it's not mandatory), shift your focus to the group discussion questions.

As you do so, remember conversations can only be as helpful as they are safe, and every safe space has four walls around it: concentration, curiosity, courage, and confidentiality. By concentration, I mean presence. Eliminate distractions, especially mobile devices. Be mindful of your thoughts wandering to work or home or grocery lists. When they wander, bring them back. Be curious. Open-minded. Become a student of the people you're with. Trust them to be good teachers, and try to learn everything you can. Try to show up as your authentic self and to create an environment where others are encouraged to do so as well by celebrating their strengths and having compassion for their hardships. And of course, confidentiality is essential. What is said in the group stays in the group!

GOOD QUESTIONS, GOOD CONVERSATIONS, GOOD COMPANIONSHIP

This is not one of those study guides that promises you a bunch of final answers. Instead, I promise you a bunch of good questions—questions that produce new conversations about the companionship in your life, and conversations that lead to insights about how you are already showing up well in your most important relationships and how you can show up even more wisely in the future.

In the words of the poet Rilke that began this chapter, it is best to live the questions now so that gradually, without noticing it, we might someday live into the answers. It's time to ask the questions now. To have the conversations. So that on some distant day we might live into the kind of companionship that will see us through.

Let's begin!

WEEK ONE

THE FOUR KINDS OF LOVE

- Inward (I): Reflect on your view of unconditional love and how it affects your relationships.
- Outward (O): Share your reasons for doing this study, the strengths you bring to companionship, and your hopes for the study experience.
- Upward (U): Discuss the four kinds of love, and *philia* in particular.

WHAT TO READ FOR THIS WEEK

The introduction to *True Companions*, titled "What You Need to Know."

INWARD

There is a tension between unconditional love and true companionship.

For instance, recently a friend was telling me about an ongoing project at his son's school: a service project meant to teach the students compassion and charity. My friend told me most of the young people in the class were choosing to raise money and donate to causes such as local animal shelters or the support of people in third world countries. I told him I thought that was admirable.

He told me it was driving him crazy.

He said sending money to a charitable organization or even showing up at an animal shelter for an afternoon is an act of love. Probably even an act of unconditional love. But it is also relatively easy. Instead, he had challenged his son to give himself to service that is hard, by which he meant scary and risky and, most importantly, up close. He challenged his son to dedicate himself to an ongoing helping relationship with one other human being. Within driving distance.

That, he said, is *true* companionship.

That conversation was on my mind the following morning. It had snowed the night before, and I was nursing a back injury. My wife was out in the driveway shoveling by herself while I prepared our weekly Saturday pancake breakfast for the kids. I asked my middle son, Quinn, to go out and help her. He refused, saying he was hungry and, on top of that, it was too cold to go outside. I thought about the kind of up-close love and service my friend had been talking about. I told Quinn that I know he loves his mother unconditionally. And I told him I would still love him unconditionally, even if he chose not to help his mother. But I also told him family is about more than unconditional love. It's about companionship, and companionship is a two-way street.

I pointed out that he was expecting me to treat him like a companion by making him breakfast, but he was not willing to treat his mother like a companion by helping her shovel. I asked him how he thought those decisions over time would affect the two-way street that is our companionship. I told him that there would be a dozen things he would ask of me that morning—from playing with him to caring for him—and I would probably do all of them. I asked him what he thought it would be like for me to do those things, knowing he wasn't willing to do this thing for his mother while I was injured. He stomped to his room. I went back to making the pancakes. Then, five minutes later, I heard the clump, clump, clump of snow boots walking out the back door. That, I told him thirty minutes later over pancakes, is *true* companionship.

The introduction to *True Companions* explores the possibility that unconditional love, while a beautiful and holy thing in its own right, can become more complicated when mingled with human fears and egos and agendas. We often hide behind the notion of it, get critical of others' failure to embody it, use it to avoid the hard work of relationships, and fill our bellies with it on a Saturday morning instead of getting down to work with our companions in the driveway. In *True Companions*, we explore the possibility that unconditional love is the highest kind of divine love, but true companionship is the highest kind of *human* love.

Let's reflect on your views of unconditional love.

Questions for Reading and Self-Reflection

1. When you hear the phrase "unconditional love," what comes to mind (e.g., sermons in a church, something you read somewhere, a scene from a movie, an experience in

your life)? Write down your ideas about unconditional love coming into this study, trying to filter out the ideas you've already started to read about in *True Companions*.

2. Now, having contemplated your previous experiences of unconditional love, write down your definition of it below by completing the sentence I've started for you. Remember, there is no right and wrong, there are only the experiences and ideas you have picked up along the way. "Unconditional love is _____."

3. Reflect on one experience in which this definition of unconditional love helped you to live and love from your best and truest self. Describe that experience below.

4. Reflect on one experience in which this definition of unconditional love permitted you to avoid some of the up-close work of true companionship. Describe that experience below.

5. Focus specifically on one of your most important relationships currently. If you quit hoping for and/or hiding behind
unconditional love in that relationship, and instead focused on the hard but holy work of being true companions,
how could that relationship change for the better? What
might it look like one year from now?

OUTWARD

This session's paired interview focuses on articulating your in-
terest in and hopes for the study as a whole, as well as your general
approach to and views about companionship. It will be an en-
joyable opportunity to share your strengths, hopes, values, and
vision. If you finish before the thirty minutes are over, that's totally fine. If you don't get all the way through the interview, that's
totally fine, too—it means you were discussing important things.

Questions for Reflection or Paired Interview

1. What draws you to this study?

2. Reflect on an experience or two in companionship of any
kind—a marriage, a family relationship, a friendship—
and share a story that helps me understand the unique

strengths or superpowers you bring to relationships. What happened, and what did you bring to the moment?

3. Reflect for a moment on what you value most deeply about companionship. When you are feeling best about your relationships, what important personal values are guiding you the most?

4. If we were meeting a year from now, celebrating what this book, this study, or this group has done in your life, what would we be celebrating?

5. In the longer term, if you had one wish for the way you'd increasingly show up in your most important relationships, what would it be?

6. What intentions have you set, or would you like to set, for how you show up to this study—or this group over the

course of the study—in order to make this the best experience for you and everyone else?

UPWARD

This week, we're focusing specifically on the "four loves" in the Greek language, which I describe in the introduction to *True Companions*. Here's a quick, abridged review. In each description I've put in bold the adjective that might best describe that love in the English language.

Agape love is **unconditional** love. It is the noblest love in the Greek language, a love that continues forever, even when it is mistreated. It is sacrificial, expecting nothing in return. We associate it with a loving God, and the Greeks almost always used it to describe God or "the gods," rather than humans.

Eros is **passionate** and usually fleeting. It is the chemistry felt at the beginning of a relationship, but its energy wanes over time. It is not bad, but it does need to be balanced by other kinds of love, lest it become selfish and destructively unsatisfied.

Storge is dispassionate, devoted, and quietly **loyal**. It arises naturally through family ties and group membership. It feels like a given and is often inherited. It feels like belonging to something bigger than ourselves.

Philia is the Greek word for friendship, or companionship. It includes an abiding sense of affection and liking as much as loving. It is intentionally cultivated and maintained. It is deeply

mutual. In other words, it places an emphasis on the continuous exchange of support and care. It is about humans learning how to be human together.

Questions for Reflection or Discussion

1. Of the adjectives above—*unconditional, passionate, loyal,* and *mutual*—which one speaks to you the most, and why?

2. What are the potential drawbacks of shifting the focus of your relationships from unconditional love to companionable love?

3. How might your relationships be improved by practicing mutuality instead of only striving for unconditionality?

4. As you think about the week ahead, what is one way you would show up differently for your people if you practiced *philia* instead of only aspiring to *agape* in your relationships?

WEEK TWO

GROWING QUIET BEFORE YOU GROW CLOSER

- Inward (I): Reflect on your experiences of abandonment, shame, and/or isolation, and how they are different from loneliness. Assemble your "loneliness team."

- Outward (O): Share your experiences with the hero's journey into your loneliness, including your successes and your resistance.

- Upward (U): Discuss the role of digital versus analog connection in creating relationships that can abide with us in our loneliness.

WHAT TO READ FOR THIS WEEK

Part one of *True Companions*, "Grow Quiet: Befriending Your Loneliness."

INWARD

Loneliness is one of the most misunderstood words in the English language, and it is one of the most misunderstood experiences

in the human condition. Personally, I got married in part because I believed it would make me unlonely. It didn't. Furthermore, as a couples therapist, I've discovered that even in
the most caring and connected companionship, *loneliness never
goes away for good.* To the contrary, the healthiest companions
I've known do not try to eliminate loneliness from their relationships; they try to *reveal* loneliness in their relationships. In
these relationships, loneliness isn't absent, it's simply talked
about. This is an essential shift in the way we relate to our loneliness, because it honors the nature of loneliness itself.

Loneliness is the shadow side of our uniqueness.

*You can't eliminate your loneliness because you can't eliminate your
uniqueness.* There are parts of you no one will ever be able to
understand. If you and your companions were a Venn diagram—
each of you a different circle of your own with various areas of
overlap—your loneliness would be everything about you that is
outside of the overlap with everyone else. Fortunately, as soon as
two people begin to reveal what their experience of loneliness is
like, the experience of being lonely itself becomes part of the
overlap, and thus they feel a little less lonely in the midst of the
sharing. When I discovered this truth, I couldn't wait to share it
with people. So, I did.

At first, they hated it.

I discovered very quickly that as soon as you use the word
loneliness in public, people have all sorts of misconceptions and
confusion about what it is. Specifically, I found out most people
confuse their experience of loneliness with three other painful
experiences: abandonment, shame, and isolation. So, I realized
that before you can have any sort of meaningful conversation

about loneliness, you first have to have a conversation about abandonment, shame, and isolation. Then you can talk about the potential for benevolence and beauty hidden within our loneliness. This is important stuff. You have to learn how to be lonely so you can learn how to truly be a companion, and you can't embrace the good work of being lonely until you have clarified what loneliness really is!

Questions for Reading and Self-Reflection

1. Begin again by trying to filter out the ideas you've already started to read about in *True Companions*, and record here your experience of loneliness prior to reading the book and beginning this study. Write down whatever surfaces within you. If it helps to get specific, focus on one experience of loneliness and the thoughts and feelings that went with it.

2. Recall an important "leaving" in your life, when you felt abandoned by either the subtle or the dramatic departure of a loved one. What personal strengths did you draw upon to cope with the abandonment, and how might those strengths be a reflection of your most unique and valuable parts?

3. Reflect on how, over the course of your life, your shame—the belief that you are not good enough for love and belonging—has completed the following sentence for you: "I feel lonely because _____." List the ways.

4. Now, complete the sentence one more time, but this time with the truth. For instance, you might complete it with "I am human" or "I am unique" or "there is no one else like me." Or choose one of your own!

5. Identify up to three people, places, or patterns of behavior that are leaving you isolated; for instance, people you pour into who don't tend to pour anything back into you, social groups that keep their interactions a little too superficial, or a tendency to get lost in digital media rather than scheduling face-to-face meetings with your companions. Try not to censor yourself. Be honest about what is adding extra loneliness to your life.

6a. Instead of trying to find one person who understands all of you, what if you assembled a "loneliness team"? Start by identifying some rare and unique things about you. List them below.

6b. Now, next to each, name one person who best understands that part of you. For instance, I might identify one friend who loves the sports I love, one friend who is as passionate about being a dad as I am, and one friend who likes to talk about death as much as I do (I know, weird).

6c. Once you have your list of people, choose up to six to be members of your loneliness team. Next to each of them, identify how you would like to cultivate that relationship.

OUTWARD

If you are doing this study in a larger group, I encourage you to pair up with someone different from last week. It's a great way for group members to connect more broadly and deeply. This session's paired interview focuses on clarifying the challenges and the rewards of your hero's journey toward your loneliness.

As a reminder, the stages of the hero's journey, as described in *True Companions* in relationship to loneliness, are as follows:

- *The ordinary world.* Life and business as usual, where there is no awareness of our loneliness.

- *The call to adventure.* Something causes our loneliness to stir in our depths.

- *Refusal of the call.* The things we do to resist paying attention to this stirring.

- *The mentor appears.* Someone or something nudges us to pay attention. In this case, that something might be this book and study guide.

- *Crossing the threshold.* We choose to let ourselves feel our loneliness.

- *Tests, allies, and enemies.* All sorts of crummy things come up with it, including abandonment, shame, isolation, and a renewed resistance to feeling it. But also, friends and mentors come alongside us to encourage us.

- *The inmost cave.* We fully experience and accept our basic human loneliness.

- *The reward.* We emerge from this experience with some sort of reward—for instance, the ability to be alone or quiet or still or peaceful.

- *The road back.* The bad guys from earlier reappear, tormenting us again and trying to rob us of our reward.

- *The resurrection.* Something shifts within us, and the rewards of befriending our loneliness become more real to us than all the resistance.

- A *gift for the people*. We approach our companionship in a wholly new way, not expecting it to take our loneliness away, but rather knowing we can be lonely, loved, and loving all at once.

Questions for Reflection or Paired Interview

1. What situations in your life are most likely to stir up some of your loneliness, calling you out of "the ordinary world" and into the adventure toward your loneliness?

2. In what ways do you refuse the call by distracting yourself from your loneliness, or simply staying focused on what's going on around you rather than attending to what's going on within you?

3. When you try to get quiet so you can go on your inward adventure, what internal resistance or "enemies" do you experience? If you've had success overcoming them, how have you done so?

4. If you have ever entered the inmost cave of your lone-liness, describe the experience. If you have not reached your inmost cave yet, what words do you imagine would describe the experience?

5. If you have ever experienced a resurrection moment in which a significant shift seemed to happen in your rela-tionship to your loneliness, describe how you were dif-ferent afterward. If this has not happened to you yet, but it happens to you tomorrow, how do you imagine your life will look different a year from now as a result of it?

6. If you have had moments of befriending your loneliness, how has that become a gift for your people, benefiting or maturing your places of companionship? If this moment and this gift are still in your future, how would you hope to show up differently to your relationships if you felt at peace with your loneliness?

UPWARD

In today's world, one of the greatest threats to analog compan-ionship is digital connection. As I described in *True Companions*, while there is nothing inherently bad about digital connection, it simply does not provide us with the rich rewards of analog communication and companionship. In Georgetown University computer scientist Cal Newport's book *Digital Minimalism* (New York: Portfolio/Penguin, 2019), he reviews research showing that digital connection does not exacerbate loneliness, depression, and anxiety, as long as it is balanced by healthy levels of analog communication. However, digital connection is taking up more and more space in our lives and crowding out our analog moments. Newport exhorts us to identify our highest values when it comes to companionship and to ask ourselves, "Is digital connection the best way to honor those values?"

Today, let's talk about the role of digital connection in our lives and our companionship.

Questions for Reflection or Discussion

1. How much do you use social media, and for what purposes? At the end of a typical day, do you feel social media served you, or did you serve it?

2. In what ways do digital media (e.g., social media, web browsing, news consumption) and your devices encroach upon your analog companionship?

3. What have you done to put boundaries on your digital world so you can be more present with your people?

4. When you abstain from social media and/or digital device usage (or imagine doing so), are you more likely to become aware of your experiences of abandonment, shame, isolation, or loneliness? If so, when you are at your best, how do you respond to those experiences?

5. If you were to abstain from mobile device and media usage for an extended period—to the extent possible given your career and commitments—how would you want to use the free time and presence to more intentionally engage your companions in the analog world?

6. What "fences" would you like to put around your use of your devices and digital media on an ongoing basis, and who could you invite to hold you accountable for doing so?

GROWING STRONG
BY GROWING WISER

WHAT TO EXPECT FROM THIS WEEK

- Inward (I): Reflect on the origins of your need to protect yourself, and begin to explore the moment of choice between protection and connection.

- Outward (O): Explore more deeply the nine protections, and identify your successes in pushing past them.

- Upward (U): Discuss the nuances of the nine protections and begin to develop a vision for building on your successes so you can live increasingly connected rather than protected with your people.

WHAT TO READ FOR THIS WEEK

Part two of *True Companions*, "Grow Strong: Embracing Your Struggle."

INWARD

Last week, you had the courage to go on an inward journey toward your loneliness, an outward journey to discuss it, and an upward journey with the group toward a better way of relating to your loneliness, your technology, and your people. Well done! This willingness to attend to, approach, and accept your ordinary human loneliness is an essential foundation for the work we will do during this week's session—the work of embracing the struggle with our protections. The same powers of observation and self-reflection you were honing last week will help you to observe your protections before you act on them, so you can make new choices about *how* to show up in your relationships.

I often begin the marriage retreats I lead by reminding the participants of the old adage that when you get married, two become one. However, I tell them, the reason marriage—and companionship of any kind—is so complicated is that, long before the two of you became one, each one of you became two. You came into the world with one truly *connective self*. Then you got hurt. It happens to all of us. And as a result of that hurt, you created a second *protective self*. We all do that too. Your connective self is the part of you that signs up for a marriage retreat (or a study about companionship), whereas your protective self is the part of you that keeps you from truly showing up to the retreat (or study). The core of true companionship is choosing to show up with your connective self again.

I call this choice *wise vulnerability*.

Wise vulnerability has several steps to it. First, we must become more familiar with the nature of our protective self. Which particular protections does it usually use? Then, we need to practice observing our protective self at work in our everyday interactions. This is half the battle, because the part of us that observes our protective self is our connective self. Third, as we become more skilled at observing our protective self in action, our connective self will be faced with a choice. Do we continue to engage defensively, or do we show up authentically?

Finally, we have an opportunity to make a wise choice. In other words, in situations where others have not proven themselves to be generally safe and caring—a toxic work environment, an abusive relationship, or any unfamiliar situation, to name a few—the connective self may wisely choose to let the protective self do its job. In other situations, however, your connective self might decide that vulnerability is worth the risk. It is important here to acknowledge that vulnerability *always* feels risky. If it didn't come with risk, it wouldn't be called vulnerability; it would be called a no-brainer. Nevertheless, in true companionship, two people, more often than not, decide to risk it.

Questions for Reading and Self-Reflection

1. In *True Companions*, I recounted several experiences of bullying in my childhood that triggered the creation of my protective self. Give yourself the permission and space now to recall one or two of the more hurtful experiences in your history. Describe the experience(s) below.

2. Describe how you began protecting yourself more after the experience(s).

3. One of the more common ways of protecting ourselves is *hiding*—for instance, staying silent, acting happy, or becoming someone we're not to get the acceptance we want. What is your most frequently used method of hiding, and when is the first time you can remember using it?

4. In addition to hiding, another common way to protect ourselves is *fighting*—for instance, verbal and/or physical aggression, fantasies of revenge, or a tendency to be critical and judgmental. Recall one time you protected yourself by becoming more aggressive, even if it only played out within you. Describe what happened.

5. In addition to hiding and fighting, *elevating* is another way to protect our connective selves from more hurt, and it may include establishing power and control, building achievements and accomplishments, stockpiling resources and riches, or pretending we're better than other people. How do you depend on these kinds of things to feel safe and satisfied? Describe your attachment to these things.

6. Describe one time when you successfully chose connection over protection. Did your companion at that time
reward your vulnerability or punish it? Was there value for
you in showing up connectively, regardless of the outcome?

OUTWARD

During your inward journey this week, you reflected on your
general pattern of protections. During this session's paired interview, we focus on the nine specific protections discussed in
True Companions. Here's a summary:

- *Anger.* When we are threatened, our nervous system becomes aroused, preparing us for action. We have two choices:
  fight or flight. Anger or anxiety. Aggression or evacuation.
  Oftentimes, we choose anger because it feels safer but also,
  even more so, because we don't want to flee. We want to
  stay, but anger feels like the only safe way to do so.

- *Peacefaking.* True peacemaking is the creation of wholeness
  and connection through two or more people showing up
  with their true voices in a way that is both authentic and
  respectful of the other. Peacefaking is what happens when
  we suppress our true voice in order to avoid "conflict."

- *Certainty.* Having unshakable beliefs, refusing to entertain
  doubt, knowing what others must be thinking, assuming
  you understand their motivations—these are all ways of

feeling in control, because uncertainty and the unpredictability of true connection feel a lot less safe.

- *Yessing.* Yessing is the tendency to say yes to every request without first filtering it through your true, connective self. This can look like peacefaking, but the function is quite different: peacefaking is usually intended to avoid disagreement, but yessing is intended to avoid abandonment. We say yes to everything in the hopes of keeping our companions around.

- *Competition.* Competition is the ultimate form of elevation, and it can become a habitual way of protecting. In other words, every relationship and every interaction is viewed through the lens of win versus loss. Instead of trying to get into true connection, we focus exclusively on getting into the winner's circle. Unfortunately, the winner's circle is a very isolated place.

- *Withdrawal.* As I write in *True Companions,* "One of the best ways to protect against the natural but challenging give-and-take of a relationship is to pretend you aren't in one." There are three primary forms of withdrawal from companionship. Secrets are our way of keeping a part of us out of the relationship. Silence is a way of withdrawing from challenging communication and connection. And separation—or the erection of too-high boundaries—is a way of withdrawing from the hard work of coexistence.

- *Fixing.* The desire to fix things is a good thing. It produces important progress in our lives and for our world. However, it can become a problem unto itself if it is used as a way to protect against the gritty work of companioning. It is easier to fix than to feel. Fixing is a way of putting something into the past, whereas feeling is a way of wading into the present with the people we love, even if that present is unpleasant.

- *Helicoptering.* Helicoptering is the opposite of fixing, in a way. Fixing is about solving problems that have happened, whereas helicoptering is about preventing them before they can happen. We protect ourselves from pain and discomfort by living according to the old adage "An ounce of prevention is worth a pound of cure."

- *Excitement.* The pursuit of interesting things is not a bad thing, but it can become a protective thing when it gets out of balance in companionship. Much of companionship is ordinary, routine, and repetitive. It is in the mundane, actually, that our love grows best and our commitment to growing together is solidified. When we value excitement above everything else, it protects us from entering into this connective space.

Questions for Reflection or Paired Interview

1. Which of the nine protections have you witnessed yourself using, and what does your most dominant protection look like when you use it in relationships?

2. Is there one protection that you cannot relate to at all? Why do you think you have no inclination to use it for protection?

3. Is there one protection that bothers you the most when someone you care about uses it in your relationship with them? Why do you think you have such a negative reaction to that type of protection?

4. Choose a relationship that is particularly important to you. How do you think your companionship with that person would improve if you stopped drawing on your protection(s) and instead focused on truly connecting?

UPWARD

Today's group discussion expands on this week's reflections and paired interview by focusing on the nine core ways of connecting. Here, I've summarized for you the antidotes described in *True Companions* for each protection.

- *Anger.* Instead of always acting on your anger, talk only about your fears. Try not to have a conversation of substance unless it is to talk about your anxiety rather than your anger.

- *Peacefaking.* Instead of avoiding conflict by quieting down, transform your conflict into true peacemaking by speaking up, while respecting your companion's voice as well.

- *Certainty.* Instead of being certain about everything, become curious about something, especially the thoughts, feelings, and behaviors of your companions. Instead of acting like a professor, become a student again.

- *Yessing.* Practice setting boundaries by saying no. Imagine that requests are suggestions, not requirements. Create space to be alone with yourself.

- *Competition.* Practice presence, being, non-doing. Engage in regular mindfulness, meditation, and prayer practices that help you to trade in competition for contemplation.

- *Withdrawal.* Catch yourself keeping small secrets and share them. Stay engaged in conversation five minutes longer than usual. Tell your companion about the experience of doing so. Look for opportunities to intertwine your lives, rather than living in parallel.

- *Fixing.* Catch yourself jumping to fixing, and make space for feeling. Instead of trying to cure, give your energy to care. Be intentional about empathizing. Explicitly create solution-free zones or discussions in your relationship.

- *Helicoptering.* Let something break. Let someone you love fall down. Be there to fix it or to help them up, but don't do so compulsively. Ask yourself if it needs to be fixed. Give them a chance to get up on their own first. Instead of trying to prevent every mess, intentionally create a few. This is called *play.*

- *Excitement.* Look for opportunities to compromise between excitement and boredom. Choose several ordinary, repetitive rituals that you want to commit yourself to in your relationships. Sacrifice something you find interesting in order to follow through on these.

Questions for Reflection or Discussion

1. Based on the nine suggested connections above, what is one specific thing you would like to do differently in your relationships to trade in your protections for connection?

2. When you have had success choosing connection over protection, what did you do to create the space to respond wisely rather than reactively, and how did it turn out?

3. Think of a time when you challenged a companion's protections, rather than struggling against your own. How did that approach affect your relationship? What helps you to resist the temptation to focus on your companion's protections and instead stay focused on the way you show up?

4. How might you encourage your companions to work on their own protections so you don't have to do the work for them?

5. What intentions would you like to set this week for engaging in wise vulnerability, which is to say creating the space for observing your protections and then choosing at least one moment in one relationship in which to trade your protection for connection?

WEEK FOUR

GROWING OLD WITH YOUR FRAGILITY PRIMED

- Inward (I): Reflect on your experience of death and dying, and the nature of your relationship to time and mortality.

- Outward (O): Develop a vision for how your priorities and focus might shift if they were guided by the priming of your fragility.

- Upward (U): Practice the priming of your fragility and debrief the experience together.

Part three of *True Companions*, "Grow Old: Cherishing Your Time."

INWARD

I hope since our last session you have been able to observe even more mindfully those moments of choice in your relationships—those moments in which you can move in the direction of protection or connection—and I hope you're finding opportunities to choose connection. This week's session focuses on another kind of choice, one that is just as important for your companionship, if not more so: the choice to think about death or not.

In *True Companions*, I briefly describe a convincing body of research showing that if we are not focused on how fragile we are, we will not focus on the values, priorities, and goals that are so essential to building the companionship we want. To summarize, young people tend to focus their lives on achievement, accumulation, and expansion, whereas the elderly tend to focus their lives on presence, enjoyment of ordinary pleasures, and deepening their existing companionship. However, the shift in values is not due to age or experience, as we often assume. It is due to something else: the elderly are more aware of their fragility.

When we are aware of our finitude and the fragility of our lives, true companionship becomes one of our highest values. Without that awareness, regardless of our age, it is almost impossible to bring a perspective to our relationships that will result in deeper commitment and connection. In other words, no matter how good-hearted you are, if you aren't guided by a sense of your mortality, your values will drift toward things that grow your footprint in the world, rather than things that help you grow satisfyingly old with your companions. So, in this session, we are going to spend some time reflecting on our mortality, becoming more aware of our fragility, and setting intentions for our relationships according to the values that arise in the midst of this experience.

Questions for Reading and Self-Reflection

1. Reflect on your first experience of mortality. Was it in relation to a friend or family member, an acquaintance, a beloved pet, or something or someone else? How did it impact you?

2. Recall your interactions with those who were around you in the midst of that loss. Were you encouraged to partic-ipate in the experience and rituals around the passing, or were you shielded from fully experiencing the loss?

3. What was your most recent brush with your own mortality, or that of someone close to you? What does your response to that experience tell you about your current relationship to mortality? Do you feel comfortable thinking about death, or do you try to avoid attending to it?

4. Life often presents us with moments in which our fragility might be primed, if we allow it. When you avoid attending to those moments, what are your methods of avoidance,

or how do you avoid thinking about death and mortality in general?

5. If you have ever allowed your fragility to be primed and to positively influence your companionship, describe below how you showed up differently to a relationship, or your relationships in general, as a result.

OUTWARD

During your inward journey this week, you reflected on your experience of, and relationship to, mortality. In this week's paired interview, we will build upon that reflection by focusing in more depth on what your life might look like and how you might show up to your people differently if you allowed yourself to be guided by an awareness of your mortality.

Questions for Reflection or Paired Interview

1. If your fragility were primed more frequently, what personal values and pursuits would feel less important to you? What values would be elevated?

2. With your fragility primed, how would you want to act upon the elevated values you just described? In other words, what would you *do* differently in your relationships?

3. Think about how your people look, how they sound, how they smell (at their best!), how they feel, and so on. What will you miss about them when their bodies are gone?

4. What activities do you enjoy doing the most with your companions? In what situations are you most likely to laugh out loud with them?

5. What things do you want to "miss out on" (i.e., eliminate, or at least minimize, such as social media) so that you can show up more attentively for your people?

UPWARD

This week we're going to begin our group discussion by doing something a little different. Instead of jumping right into conversation, we're going to take about five minutes to do an exercise together. This exercise is intended to prime your fragility a little bit. Choose a group leader to move you through this exercise. If you are doing this study on your own, you are the group leader! Take a couple of minutes for everyone to read all the way through the exercise.

Now, make yourselves comfortable and settle in.

The group leader begins by giving the following instructions. "Take a deep cleansing breath, breathing in to the count of four and out to the count of four. [Wait approximately thirty seconds to let people establish a breathing rhythm. Then, continue with the following.] Now, just breath naturally. Take about a minute to do nothing else but attend to your breath. Find a spot in your body—your lungs, abdomen, mouth, or nose—where the breathing sensations are most vivid, and bring all of your awareness to this place as you breathe."

After a minute or two of breathing like this, the group leader can bring this time of mindful breathing to a close by reading the following prompt: "Now, identify one companion who is particularly important to you, someone you hope to grow old with. Listen for something deep within telling you the person you want to focus on." After thirty seconds, ask for confirmation through a show of hands that everyone has designated their companion.

Then, the group leader reads aloud the following prompt: "What is the one thing you'd want to say to your companion if you only had one more chance?" Give the group members about five minutes to reflect on this question and write down what comes to mind. I highly recommend playing the song "Special" by a band called Jukebox the Ghost while group members are reflecting. It's not mandatory; it's just beautiful.

I've had two very different real-life experiences with regard to this question, both of which I shared in *True Companions*. When I was in college, my beloved grandfather died suddenly, before I got a chance to thank him for his companionship, and before I got a chance to take him up on his offer to play one more round of golf together. It has taken me many years to be at peace with that missed opportunity. More recently, a man named Dave approached me at my book table after a speaking event. The urge arose within me to tell him that he had kind eyes. I usually ignore those urges, but this time I didn't. Dave died several days later. His friends tell me that he died knowing he had kind eyes. I'm so glad I told Dave that while I still had the chance.

What would you say to your companion if you only had one more chance?

Questions for Reflection or Discussion

The questions I've provided below apply to the above exercise, and they assume you have completed it. However, this week in particular, follow the conversation where it leads, as long as that direction is into a greater appreciation for your finitude and fragility.

1. Which companion did you choose to focus on during the exercise? What did you choose to say to them, and why?

2. If you continued to maintain awareness of your and your companions' fragility in this way, how would the quality of your time with them improve? What would you do more of and what would you do less of?

3. What intentions do you want to set for attending to the things you most appreciate about your companions? How many times do you want to express that appreciation to them over the next week?

4. What intentions do you want to set for engaging in the activities you most enjoy with your companions over the coming year? For instance, can you identify one small thing you want to do more consistently with them, or one big thing you want to put on the calendar?

5. What is one activity or pursuit you would like to eliminate from your life so you can have more time to engage in your highest values with your companions? What is one step you could take toward doing so?

WEEK FIVE

WHO LOVED YOU INTO BEING?

- Inward (I): Host a "timeless reunion" of your own and reflect on the exercise.

- Outward (O): Cultivate a new appreciation for the companions who have influenced your life for the better, in both small and significant ways.

- Upward (U): Reflect on the study experience in general and, if you are in a group, the group experience specifically.

The final letter in *True Companions*, "A Timeless Reunion."

INWARD

It's hard to believe we have already arrived at our final session. I'm grateful you've come this far with me. This week, we're going to go just a little farther by imagining the kind of timeless reunion that I write about in the final letter to my wife in *True Companions*. If you haven't already read it, go do so now. Are you back? Good. Are you ready to spend some time reflecting on the kaleidoscope of companionship that has been your life? Good!

You might remember that, at the beginning of *True Companions*, I told a story of an elderly couple in the line opposite me at a Thanksgiving buffet. Well, last year, we went to the same buffet for our Thanksgiving meal. This time, I didn't see a couple like that. However, after the meal, I did see something that touched me deeply—our family went to see the movie about Mr. Rogers titled *A Beautiful Day in the Neighborhood* starring Tom Hanks (directed by Marielle Heller [Burbank, CA: TriStar Pictures, 2019]). There is a scene in that movie in which Mr. Rogers is sitting in a restaurant with the tormented protagonist, Lloyd Vogler, and he asks Lloyd to do something with him.

He says, "We'll just take a minute and think about all the people who loved us into being." Then they grow silent, along with everyone in the restaurant—and presumably everyone in the theater—while Tom Hanks looks directly into the camera as a silent invitation for moviegoers to engage in the exercise as well. I guess I'm doing something sort of like that here. Through the pages of this study guide, I'm looking at you and saying, "Let's be silent for just a little while to think about all the people who loved us into being." We're going to do so by imagining a timeless reunion of our companions. I really do believe something like this is happening within us all of the time. However, we rarely attend to it. So, would you go on one more inward journey with me by showing up to the reunion that is already under way within you?

When you're ready, let's start.

Find a quiet place where you can be uninterrupted for fifteen to thirty minutes. Begin by imagining the setting for your reunion. Remember, you don't need to create it; it already exists within you. Just listen and watch for the scene that presents itself. Mine was in a park. My wife's was on the back porch of her grand-mother's house. Yours can be in any place of your choosing, or any place that chooses you.

Once you've settled on the setting, imagine yourself sitting quietly in that space. Perhaps there are some companions already there with you who have helped you set up the party. Perhaps you did it alone. Both are perfectly okay. Now, notice you hear a car approaching. It arrives and someone gets out. Spend some time noticing who it is. Greet them. Create some space around you and within you to welcome them. Then, notice that other people are beginning to arrive, a long line of people who have, in Mr. Rogers's words, "loved you into being." Some of them are probably expected, but some may surprise you. Some may still be alive, but some of them will almost certainly have passed. Some may live a great distance from you now, while some may live right in your neighborhood. Just let them come. Don't censor yourself. Anyone is allowed, so long as they have played at least some small role in your kaleidoscope. Let the reunion last as long as you want. Once it is over, create just a little more time and space to reflect on and respond to the questions below.

Questions for Reading and Self-Reflection

1. Record whatever details from your timeless reunion you want to be sure to remember. Write down as much or as little as you wish.

2. Which guest at your reunion was most expected? How did it feel to see them and interact with them? What role has this companion played in loving you into being?

3. Which guest at your reunion was most unexpected, and why? What is/was it about your companionship with them that resulted in their "invitation" to the reunion?

4. If someone did not show up at your reunion that you expected to be there, in all likelihood, it's because you didn't have enough time to get all the way through the line of arrivals, or there were some stragglers who didn't show up on time. List those people here now, and set the intention of attending to them the next time you host a timeless reunion.

5. Which guest or guests are still most present in your day-to-day life right now? What did your reunion show you about how you value your companionship with them? How might you share this with them or express it to them?

OUTWARD

In the last chapter of *True Companions*, I reflect again on the differences between unconditional love, *agape*, and true companionship, *philia*. During this week's paired interview, we revisit those contrasts. More specifically, in the book I described a scene at my church, in which two lines of congregants were moving forward to receive Communion, but one line was held up by an elderly man at the front who forgot where he was. Consider your experience of your timeless reunion, along with the following passage, as you enter into this week's final paired interview.

"In the bread and the wine, I saw the gift of *agape*—the divine and unconditional love at which we all hope to arrive. In this waiting, though, I saw the gift of *philia*. Our lives are a long line moving steadily toward *agape*.

Philia is the love that waits with us.

It is a patient witness, and it can be many witnesses—those from our past who we have lost, those from our present who we have for now, and those from our future who we will one day come to know. In some mysterious way, as we slowly approach the gift of *agape*, they all stand there in line with us. Watching. Witnessing. Waiting. And this waiting is true companionship."

Questions for Reflection or Paired Interview

1. When you began this book and this study, did you think of *agape* love as "better" than *philia,* and has that opinion changed over the course of this study?

2. Reflect on the people who showed up at your timeless reunion. How did some of them "love you into being" through companionship instead of unconditional love?

3. If you think of *agape* as the gift of unconditional love that we get to finally, fully experience in the life after this one, and *philia* as the love that waits with us, how does that affect your appreciation for those who are waiting with you right now but perhaps not able to love you unconditionally?

4. *True Companions* concludes by returning to the idea that true companionship is about committing to "figuring it out" with our people. What ordinary life hurdles do you want to recommit to figuring out with some of the people in your life right now?

5. How would you like to express this commitment to them in words or action?

UPWARD

Finally, we have arrived at our last chance to reflect on this study and to share our appreciation for the growth and (if you've done this in a group) the group. I can't continue on with you from here, but you can continue on with each other and, of course, with yourself.

Blessings upon your journey.

Questions for Reflection or Discussion

1. What is one way this book and study have challenged you to grow most over the last five sessions? Was it in the area of growing quiet, growing strong, or growing old, or some combination of the three?

2. How are you going to show up differently for your people as a result of this growth? How might you already be doing so?

3. What is one thing you now appreciate more about your companions—including those here in the group, if you are studying this with someone—as a result of having completed this journey?

4. A year from now, if we were to celebrate the way your relationships have evolved as a result of what you've learned and experienced here, what would we be celebrating?

5. Now that you've completed the study, is there any other companion (or companions) you would like to work through the study with again?

ABOUT THE AUTHOR

KELLY FLANAGAN is a writer, speaker, and clinical psychologist who enjoys helping people cultivate true companionship and a true calling with their most authentic self. He is the founder of Artisan Clinical Associates in Naperville, Illinois, a therapy practice serving the needs of individuals, couples, and families in the Chicagoland area. He is a sought-after speaker to churches, marriage retreats, hospital systems, corporate leadership, entrepreneurs, and professional sports teams, and he hosts an annual private retreat focused on personal formation and relationship health.

In 2005, Kelly earned a PhD in clinical psychology from Penn State University and went into private practice. In 2012, he began his now-popular blog at drkellyflanagan.com, which has reached millions of readers. He continues to blog monthly about topics related to personal growth, spiritual formation, and relationship flourishing. His writing has been featured in *Reader's Digest* and *The Huffington Post*, and he has appeared on *The Today Show*. In 2017, he published his first book, *Loveable: Embracing What Is Truest About You So You Can Truly Embrace Your Life*.

Kelly is married to another clinical psychologist named Kelly, and their three children are in the eleventh, seventh, and fifth grades. They live in a small, rural town outside of Chicago, where they are learning to slow down, be present to one another, and enjoy their companionship while they can.

To connect with Kelly, go to his
website at drkellyflanagan.com, where you can
subscribe to his monthly newsletter, contact him for speaking,
and get your free copy of his fifty-two week plan for
embracing your most authentic self, cultivating true
companionship, and clarifying your calling.